Your Amazing Itty Bitty™ Book For Answered Prayers

15 Steps to Bring Your Prayers Into Reality

Dr. Joyce H. Craft has simplified the steps created by Dr. Ernest Holmes, the founder of Scientific Prayer Treatment, who has shared that there is a Power for good in the Universe available for your use. You can apply the Scientific Process of prayer to acquire good in your life.

Using the power of prayer, you can learn:

- How to recognize the Power within
- How to access Universal Mind, Spirit and Intelligence
- How to meditate and do Scientific Prayer Treatment
- How to recognize the limitless power that is behind the attainment of your highest good.

Practice the steps in this guidebook and experience what the power of prayer can do for you today.

Your Amazing Itty Bitty™ Book For Answered Prayers

15 Steps to Bring Your Prayers into Reality

**Dr. Joyce Hutchinson Craft
EdD, RScP**

Published by Itty Bitty™ Publishing
A subsidiary of S & P Productions, Inc.

Copyright © 2020 **Dr. Joyce Hutchinson Craft**

All rights reserved. No part of this book may be reproduced or transmitted in any form or by any means, electronic or mechanical, including photocopying, recording or by any information storage and retrieval system, without written permission of the publisher, except for inclusion of brief quotations in a review.

Printed in the United States of America

Itty Bitty Publishing
311 Main Street, Suite D
El Segundo, CA 90245
(310) 640-8885

ISBN: 978-1-950326-69-3

Dedication

This book is dedicated to all those who are on a personal journey for getting their prayers answered.

May the steps presented in the process of Scientific Prayer Treatment and my suggestions for enhancing your application bring great joy in having your prayers answered.

"With God All Things Are Possible."

~ *Dr. Joyce*

Stop by our Itty Bitty™ website Directory to find interesting information from our experts.

www.IttyBittyPublishing.com

Table of Contents

Introduction
- Step 1. Recognition
- Step 2. Unification
- Step 3. Declaration
- Step 4. Thanksgiving
- Step 5. Release
- Step 6. Requirements for Effective Use of Scientific Prayer Treatment
- Step 7. Take Action and Collaborate with Mind/God Now
- Step 8. The Role of Acceptance
- Step 9. The Role of Faith
- Step 10. The Role of Meditation
- Step 11. The Role of Mental Equivalents
- Step 12. The Role of Practicing the Presence
- Step 13. What Causes Scientific Prayer Treatment to Work
- Step 14. The Role of Conscious Mind
- Step 15. The Role of Subconscious Mind

Introduction

When you complete this Itty Bitty™ Book, you will have the tools needed for your prayers to be answered.

Dr. Ernest Holmes, the Founder of Scientific Prayer Treatment, taught and demonstrated how to get your prayers answered. He shared that there is a Power for good in the Universe and you can use it. You can use prayer to get whatever you desire to bring into your life and also into the lives of others. It is a Scientific Process and your responsibility is to learn the principles and apply them to acquire your good.

In this Itty Bitty™ Book, you will learn what the principles are and how to use them.

You are also presented with measures to reinforce your ability to apply the principles and rely on that Power to answer your prayers.

Yes indeed "Ask and ye shall receive."

Step 1
Recognition

The first step in the process is Recognition.

1. What are you recognizing? You are recognizing the Power that is behind getting your prayers answered.
2. In his book, The Science of Mind, Dr. Ernest Holmes refers to the Living Presence within, which is the Father in Heaven.
3. Dr. Holmes also said you should "recognize It as the one and only power in the Universe."
4. It is "Universal Mind, Spirit and Intelligence that is the origin of everything."
5. Additionally, he gives the traits of this power as:
   Omniscience – All Knowing.
   Omnipotence – All Powerful.
   Omnipresence – Everywhere Present.
6. He added that, It is a "Power for Good," which surrounds you and in which you are immersed.
7. Holmes summarized It as Universal Mind Spirit and Intelligence that is the origin of everything.

Recognition Exercise

- You need to start by recognizing that there is a Power for good.
- The great news is that you can use It to bring whatever good you desire into your life.
- Recognition of God/Universal Mind is as necessary to your spirit as food is to the health of your physical body.
- It is the source you approach when you pray, meditate and do Scientific Prayer Treatment, because It is that Power that creates whatever exists or is created.
- This is the source with which you interact when you express what you want to come into in your life—It is the source of your existence and the creator of everything including you.
- When you commune or pray, you are aware of what you are praying to and thus bring credence to your endeavor.
- You are recognizing the limitless Power that is behind the attainment of your highest good.

Step 2
Unification

The second step in the process is unification. With what are you unifying?

1. Dr. Holmes refers to Unification *as, "The oneness of God and man."*
2. Jesus the Teacher taught – "that they may all be one, even as Thou, Father, art in me and I in Thee and they also in us."
3. Unification is where you affirm your oneness with God and consciously embrace and link up with It and feel Its love.
4. You are made in the image and likeness of God and inherit all of Its attributes.
5. Reflect on the teaching of Jesus when He said, "I can of mine own self do nothing… The Father that dwells within… He doeth the work."
6. Turn within and feel God's presence.

Unification Exercises:

- You are consciously aware that there is no separation from God.
- As you acknowledge your unification with God, you become a conduit through which God operates.
- This gives you the authority and responsibility to speak your word, to declare with faith that "With God all things are possible."
- You embrace it, and you enjoy your demonstration of unifying with God.
- Unification is necessary because you realize that God is at your center which gives power to the request you made.
- Say to yourself:
  I embrace the presence of God.
  It embraces me and we are one.
  I feel my oneness with God.
  And so, it is.

Step 3
Declaration

Dr. Holmes puts Declaration in the context of "Speaking your word," requesting what you would like to come into your life.

1. In this step you are making a request to God for what you desire.
2. There is a subtlety here.
   Think of the word desire. It means: "out from the Father."
   What you desire or declare is actually prompted by something coming from Universal Mind - God in you.
   In this process you are realizing your oneness with God and are listening to what is coming from God Itself. In this oneness realize that your request is actually prompted by God because He knows your needs and is ready to supply it.
3. Declare, echo back to God what It communicates to you – your desire.
4. Ernest Holmes said, "Legitimate desire is the voice of Spirit within you trying to indicate that the thing you desire is already on its way to you."
5. Declare what you desire and expect to receive it.

Declaration Exercises:

- Think about what you would like to come into your life.
- Listen to your Inner Voice.
- Choose well because you will get what you ask for.
- Speak your word – echo back to God what you are seeking, which emanated from God.
- Embody it as if you already see it, have it and are experiencing it.
- With faith and confidence expect God to bring into your life that which is for your highest good.
- Your word has power. It sets God in motion.
- No coercion is necessary. It creates what it initiated from Its own knowingness.
- Be reminded, Jesus said "Ask and it shall be given unto you."
- Reflect on this passage, "and all things whatsoever ye shall ask in prayer, believing ye shall receive."

Step 4
Thanksgiving

The principle underlying Step 4 is that you are *already* receiving what you requested and so you express gratitude for it.

1. The outcome or demonstration might not be evident as yet, but your faith and trust in the principle are so complete, you can thank God, Universal Mind that it is already accomplished. What faith Jesus had in this principle!
2. He gave thanks before declaring his intentions. He began his activities with "Father, I thank thee that you hearest me always." Then he proceeded to heal the sick, raise the dead or feed five thousand.
3. These activities of thanksgiving, praising and rejoicing are creating within your consciousness the confirmation that your prayer is being answered.
4. You are reassuring yourself that you believe God is making good Its promise because your request grew out of the consciousness you felt while you communed with God.
5. God, Universal Mind is creating, and you need not be anxious about its manifestation.

Thanksgiving Exercises:

Develop a strong trust that there is a power in the Universe which has the limitless ability to create what you declared.

- Trust the Law which demonstrates that "You receive as you believe."
- Accept the fact that the Law is working and there is nothing that can alter It.
- Remind yourself of the scriptural verse "Before you ask, I will answer."
- Develop an attitude of gratitude. Imagine that which you are seeking is already being manifested.

Inspirational Thought for Thanksgiving

"Father, I thank Thee that Thou hast heard me."
John 11:41

I perceive that my desire is being manifested. I accept my good and with a grateful heart, I say thank you, thank you, thank you God, Universal Mind.

Step 5
Release

Step 5 of Scientific Prayer Treatment is releasing your prayer to the Power that you recognized when you began the process. You now let go and let that Power, Universal Mind do Its work.

1. Having surrendered your request to God and trusting the Law and Power of God to create what you declared from the depth of your consciousness, you need to let go of how it will be attained.
2. Turn it completely over to God and let It manifest your good into your life.
3. This is your reliance on faith and trust in God.
4. Remember that what you declared is the urge that came out from God through you and hence it must be for your highest good.
5. Jesus the Teacher reminds us that, "It is not I but the Father that doeth the work." So, release your choice and let God/Universal Mind create for you. You have completed the cycle by acknowledging that God/Universal Mind is the Intelligent Knower and the Powerful Executor.

Release Exercises:

- Release your declaration and let God/Universal Mind, create it for you.
- God/Universal Mind is the Intelligent Knower and the Powerful Executor.
- It responds to what you declared and brings it into fruition.

What does Release mean to you?

- Take a few minutes to think about releasing your declaration to God/Universal Mind.
- What does it mean to you?
- What resonates with you?
- For example, "Thank you Universal Presence. I release my treatment to You knowing that my word will not return to me void. It is done as I believe. I let go and let God. And so, it is."

Step 6
Requirements for Effective Use of Scientific Prayer Treatment

The basic premise of Scientific Prayer Treatment is that you are surrounded by, and immersed in, the Universal Mind/God. It reacts to your thinking and the depth of your belief. It is a Power for good and you can use it to bring whatever you desire. It requires that you:

1. Acknowledge the source of your supply which is God/Universal Mind.
2. Surrender to Its Consciousness and unite with Its power.
3. In this consciousness declare to Universal Mind what you desire.
4. Listen to what God/Universal Mind imparts to you. It knows your highest good. Echo back to God/Universal Mind what comes from within you.
5. Accept and be thankful that God/Universal Mind honors its promise to give you what you requested.
6. Release the responsibility for creating the answer to what you declared to God/Universal Mind. As you await the outcomes, be joyful and know that which is for your highest good is being created for you.

Effective Use of Scientific Prayer Treatment Exercises:

To reap the benefits of Scientific Prayer Treatment you must:

- Learn the Principle.
- Apply it.
- Cooperate with the nature of the Principle and let It do Its work.
- Be steadfast in expecting the logical outcome.
- Be thankful that you are manifesting what you desired.
- Know that God/Universal Mind is the Doer, so let go and let God do Its work.
- Take action and apply what Universal Mind directs you to do.
- Receive it gratefully.
- Let go and allow God to create your good.

Step 7
Take Action and Collaborate with Mind/God Now

There is a saying about applying Scientific Prayer Treatment – "When you treat, move your feet." In other words, take action to actualize your goals, knowing that Mind/God is creating situations and leading people to support your efforts.

Scientific Prayer Treatment requires that you:

1. Recognize and acknowledge the source of your supply – God/Universal Mind.
2. Surrender to Its consciousness and unite with Its power.
3. Bring your request to God, Universal Mind and declare what you desire. Listen to what God imparts to you, as insight for your next experience. Echo back to God the request that comes from within you, from your Divine consciousness. Embody this, declaring it with faith and confidence.
4. Accept and be thankful that God honors Its promise to give what you declared.
5. Let go or release to God, the response-ability for creating the answer. As you wait its manifestation, be joyful and know that your highest good is being created for you.

Take action and Collaborate with Mind/God Now Exercises:

Take action and do a Scientific Prayer Treatment. Here is a simple sample of a Scientific Prayer Treatment:

Prosperity

- God is all-knowing, all-powerful and is present everywhere.
- It is a Power for good which surrounds me and in which I am immersed. It is the source of my supply.
- As I draw near to God, God draws near to me. We unite and become one.
- In this oneness, I speak my word declaring that: What I desire God to bring into my life, is brought into my life right now. (Name what you desire.)
- I claim my good with deep gratitude and a prayer of thanksgiving.
- With faith and loving acceptance, I release my desires to God, knowing that He promised "Before you call I will answer."

        Thank you, Father.
        I let go and let God.
          And so, it is.

Step 8
The Role of Acceptance:

There are five additional Practices to enhance your proficiency. They are: Acceptance, Faith, Meditation, Mental Equivalents and Practicing the Presence. By applying these tools, you allow the Power of God to express in and through you and you receive your highest good.

The Role of Acceptance:

Acceptance is the behavior in which you are convinced that God is working on your behalf to deliver your highest good.
The act of acceptance is based on these basic principles that:

1. God accepted your declaration and is ready, willing and able to deliver your request.
2. God is your supply for whatever you declare.
3. Your word or what you declared has power – it has the power of God because you unified with God and it is therefore accorded God's power.
4. The power of your word activates the Law to work on your behalf.

These Practices Reinforce the Power of Acceptance Exercises:

Dr. Ernest Holmes reminds us that:
"Our mental acceptance should be filled with conviction, warmth, color and imagination. The creative power responds to feelings more quickly than to any other mental attitude."

Other concepts that reinforce the practice of Acceptance are:

- "Ask and ye shall receive."
- "Seek and ye shall find."
- "Knock and it shall be opened unto you."
- "With God all things are possible."
- "As you believe so shall you receive."

Step 9
The Role of Faith

Faith is belief in the unseen. It is critical that you believe that Mind/God responds to what you declare or ask for. In Scientific Prayer Treatment, Faith plays a very important role in the Declaration step.

1. It is critical that you believe Mind/God responds to your declaration or what you desire.
2. Believe that your request will be granted.
3. Be willing to surrender to the Power of God.
4. It requires complete trust in that Power and that, "With God all things are Possible." Believe that God follows through in Its pleasure to give you the Kingdom – your highest good.
5. Its nature is to give, not to withhold your good.

The Role of Faith

- The Teacher Jesus told us, "All things are possible to him that believes."
- Your responsibility is to align yourself with the Power of God.
- Develop a positive conviction that the Power will perform according to Its nature.
- Reflect on the story of the healing of the Centurion servant in the Bible, where his only request was "Speak the word and my servant will be healed." Jesus marveled at his faith and said, "I say unto you, I have not found such a faith, no, not in Israel." Of course, when the Centurion arrived home, he learned that his servant was healed at the same time Jesus spoke His word.
- Accept the notion of receiving what you desire even before you actually receive it.
- Say to yourself, "With God all things are possible."

Step 10
The Role of Meditation

Dr. Ernest Holmes said, "Meditation is for the purpose of becoming receptive to the Divine Influx."

1. Through meditation you can uncover and declare your highest good as well as validate that, what you perceive as your highest good is what God intends for you.
2. It provides an opportunity for you to commune with God which is centered within you.
3. In this practice you become quiet, detach yourself from your surroundings, turn inward and tune in to the presence of God within you.
4. No coercion is necessary because Its nature is to give of Itself and to provide what It knows as your desire.
5. Understand that God already knows your desires, what is for your highest good and is willing, ready and able to supply it.

The Role of Meditation

Here is a simple Meditation for your application:

- Sit quietly in an upright position.
- Place your hands on your lap, palms up indicating a receptive attitude.
- Close your eyes, shutting out the distraction from your surroundings.
- Take a few deep breaths and as you exhale, rid yourself of any anxiety, care or concerns which may be on your mind.
- Relax in the stillness, letting the peace and love of God permeate your entire being. Imagine God's spirit flowing down through your entire being, from the crown of your head to the soles of your feet.
- Let God's spirit unite with your spirit and become one with it. You are now enveloped by its loving presence.
- As you surrender to Its power, say to yourself – "Speak Lord, your servant hears you." Listen and hear what It imparts to you.
- Be thankful and affirm, "I am renewed and refreshed as my whole being responds to your love. I am complete in your care. Thank you, God/Universal Mind."
  And so, it is.

Step 11
The Role of Mental Equivalents

In discussing Mental Equivalents, Ernest Holmes shared the following concept:
"We cannot demonstrate life beyond our mental ability to embody… If we are to draw from life what we want, we must first think it forth into life. It always produces what we think. If we want a thing we must have within ourselves the mental equivalent before we get it."

Here is a procedure to follow for desirable outcomes:

1. When you pray for what you desire you must have an image or a mental equivalent of what you desire.
2. Have in your mind's eye a picture of what you desire.
3. Express to God what you see as your desire.
4. God is ready to create what you described and will honor your request.

The Role of Mental Equivalents

It is essential that when you express to God what you desire, you bring to the request a visual or mental equivalent of what you are seeking. The following activities will enhance receiving what you ask for:

- Sit quietly and think about what you would like.
- Be specific about what your preference is to be, to do and to have. This is not a dream but something specific you would like to experience in your life.
- Form a mental picture of it. See it in your mind's eye.
- Describe it to yourself. The more details the better. You may want to write it down and or build a collage or vision board to depict what is in your mind about it.
- Focus on your goal. See it in your mind's eye. Expect it to materialize.
- Accept it and be thankful.

Step 12
The Role of Practicing the Presence

Cardinal Francis Xavier Nguyen Thuan said, *"If there is not a unifying element to your life, it will be meaningless. That element is the love of God. With it your life will change and all your actions will testify to God's presence within you."*

As you develop a relationship with God, your life becomes transformed.

1. This relationship enables you to live with a sense that you are surrounded by and immersed in a Presence that guides everything you think, say, do and are. This is what some people call, living with grace and ease.
2. You recognize that there is a power that enfolds you, energizes and frees you to live in peace, love and harmony.
3. It shows you the way to accomplish, ask for what you would like and to set your goals according to your defined purpose.
4. This is not wishful thinking, but is developing a consciousness and deliberately internalizing the unifying principle – "I will be with you always."
5. This is the consciousness that David, in the book of Psalms, allowed to guide him.

The Role of Practicing the Presence

Making Practicing the Presence of God a priority in your life, your needs will be met. Here are a few actions you may want to practice.

- Sit quietly and contemplate the nature of the Power that guides your life.
- Develop a consciousness of unification that the Presence and Power are in and around you always.
- Tap into this Presence and become one with It through meditation.
- Accept that it is with you always and as you go about your daily activities, maintain that awareness and revel in its presence.
- Practice the Presence until it becomes second nature to you and you become so proficient at it that it becomes a way of life.
- *Say this powerful affirmation (written by James Dillet Freeman) to yourself:*

"The light of God surrounds me;
The love of God enfolds me;
The power of God protects me;
The presence of God watches over me.
Wherever I am, God is!"

Step 13
What Causes Scientific Prayer Treatment to Work
(The Role of Conscious Mind)

Mind is the Power that causes Scientific Prayer Treatment to work. It is the only Power in the Universe and you are an integral part of Mind. What is true of Mind is true of you. There are two aspects of Mind. They are Conscious Mind and Sub-Conscious Mind.

Conscious Mind
1. It is The Knower – The Director.
2. It is Self – Knowing.
3. It is your thoughts.
4. It is the cause behind everything in the Universe and in your life.
5. It is the starting point for every new creation.

What Causes Scientific Prayer Treatment to Work (The Role of Conscious Mind)

Conscious Mind
- Your Conscious Mind gives directions to your Sub-Conscious Mind
- These directions are based on the desires you made when you prayed.
- Be specific about what you desire because this is what Conscious Mind conveys to Sub-Conscious Mind.

Step 14

What Causes Scientific Prayer Treatment to Work
(The Role of Sub-Conscious Mind)

1. Sub-Conscious Mind is the Law of God in action – the Executor.
2. It is the Servant of Conscious Mind.
3. It creates by following directions given by Conscious Mind.
4. There is a limitless dimension to Sub – Conscious Mind because it is continuously following directions given by Conscious Mind, The Director.
5. Jack Addington said, "The Sub-Conscious Mind is not only the keeper of the body, but the builder of the body and the builder of our lives and our affairs. The Sub-Conscious Mind knows only to take orders from Conscious Mind and carry out those orders with precision and exactitude."

What Causes Scientific Prayer Treatment to Work (The Role of Sub-Conscious Mind)

- The desire impressed on your Sub – Conscious Mind becomes the path it will follow to create the answer of your prayers.
- It is absolutely responsive to tasks given it.
- It is not judgmental or discriminating and operates in a deductive manner.
- It complies with orders and executes all directives given to it by Conscious Mind.

Step 15

How Scientific Prayer Treatment Works

When you pray and declare what you desire, it goes into Universal Mind which is ready to create your desire.

1. Your desire sets the Law of Mind into action.
2. Conscious Mind impresses on Sub-Conscious Mind what you declared.
3. Sub-Conscious Mind accepts the impressions it receives from Conscious Mind.
4. It creates, based on the impressions It receives, which is based on your declared desires.
5. Sub-Conscious Mind creates the logical outcome – the answer to your prayers.
6. It is an orderly process complying with the impression It receives:
   Affirm, "I ask and I receive, Thank you God."

How Scientific Prayer Treatment Works

- You use Conscious Mind which is the Knower/Director.
- Sub-Conscious Mind creates based on directions from Conscious Mind.
- You receive the outcome of what Sub-Conscious Mind created based on your declared desire.
- Accept your good with joy and gratitude.
- Yes, "There is a Power for good in the universe and you can use it."
- You use it by impressing on Mind what you desire to come into your life: "As you believe so shall you receive."

You've finished. Before you go…

Tweet/share that you finished this book.

Please star rate this book.

Reviews are solid gold to writers. Please take a few minutes to give us some itty bitty feedback on this book.

About The Author

Dr. Joyce Hutchinson Craft holds Bachelor and Master of Arts degrees, a Doctoral degree in education as well as certification as a Spiritual Practitioner. Dr. Joyce grew up with the motto, "With God all things are possible," which is the keystone to her life and her work. She blends education, life experience, and the Science of Mind to teach others how to attain their highest good through Scientific Prayer Treatment. Her work as an author and spiritual practitioner includes teaching and lecturing.

If you enjoyed this Itty Bitty™ book you might also like…

- **Your Amazing Itty Bitty® Book of Faith** – Kelly Smith

- **Your Amazing Itty Bitty® Gratitude Book** – Belinda Lee Cook

- **Your Amazing Itty Bitty® Relationships as a Spiritual Practice Book** – Deborah A. Gayle

Or any of the many Amazing Itty Bitty™ books available online at www.IttyBittyPublishing.com

www.ingramcontent.com/pod-product-compliance
Lightning Source LLC
Chambersburg PA
CBHW061305040426
42444CB00010B/2532